Skookum Jim

and
The Klondike Gold Rush

Chrys Salt

Indigo Dreams Publishing

First Edition: Skookum Jim and The Klondike Gold Rush
First published in Great Britain in 2020 by:
Indigo Dreams Publishing
24, Forest Houses
Cookworthy Moor
Halwill
Beaworthy
Devon
EX21 5UU
www.indigodreams.co.uk

Chrys Salt has asserted her right under the Copyright, Designs and Patents Act 1988 to be identified as the author of this work.
© 2020 Chrys Salt

ISBN 978-1-912876-29-7

British Library Cataloguing in Publication Data. A CIP record for this book can be obtained from the British Library.

Designed and typeset in Palatino Linotype by Indigo Dreams.
Cover design by Deirdre Carlisle.
Author photograph by Claire Newman Williams.
Printed and bound in Great Britain by 4edge Ltd.

Papers used by Indigo Dreams are recyclable products made from wood grown in sustainable forests following the guidance of the Forest Stewardship Council.

FOREWORD

In 1896 The Klondike Gold Rush enticed tens of thousands of people to The Yukon Territory in Northern Canada, to Dawson City and the gold fields beyond. People came from the USA and across the globe, sacrificing everything they had in an often fruitless quest for gold. Some, a very few, became rich beyond imagining, many died on the arduous journey, turned back, went home empty handed or laboured in the goldfields for The Klondike Kings – those who had struck lucky.

I visited Yukon in 2014 and travelled North with local relatives from the capital Whitehorse to the Northwest Territories Festival. While there I began to learn a little about The Gold Rush at the heart of Yukon's history. I was hooked. I started to write and in 2017 was awarded Open Lottery Funding by Creative Scotland to go back and continue my researches for this collection.

It was 'Skookum' Jim Mason (First Nation name Keish) – a member of The Tagish First Nation – along with a small party of prospectors who found gold in Rabbit Creek (renamed Bonanza) that inspired the great stampede. I like to think it was Keish's kindness in rescuing a Coast Frog stranded in a ditch and the mystery of dreams that led to their discovery.

Since I began writing and researching for this collection I have lost track of the books read, archives trawled, newspaper cuttings explored, galleries visited, journeys made. Sometimes I gleaned just a tiny slip of an idea, a snippet of information that lodged in my head planting a seed that later sprouted into a poem. I found this note in one of my many note books, heaven knows where it came from:

Everything you look at,
a bird flying,
an insect crawling,
an idea comes, an idea comes...

There are brilliant accounts of The Klondike Gold Rush from fine writers like Tapen Adney, Pierre Berton, and Jack London, and in the stories told to British poet Robert Service by prospectors in Dawson City bars. There are important archives and museums in Whitehorse and in Seattle from where many of the American prospectors set out, and impressive cultural collections in First Nation Centres in Dawson City, Whitehorse and Carcross. These poems do not purport to retell that history. That is not the province of poetry. And while it is intended to be read as a sequence it is not always chronological or factual. Did Skookum Jim ever drink in The Grand Forks Hotel? I have no idea, but when stories are passed on orally they are often embroidered, sometimes inaccurate. The 'conceit' of some of these poems is rooted in this notion.

In writing this I have sought to travel the fine line between contextualising the impact of the sudden stampede of 'get rich quick' prospectors, and adapting for a new audience the stories of the First Nation peoples who have already suffered the impacts on their livelihoods, environment, culture and way of life. Not to have reflected the legends and stories that are important to the cultures of the indigenous peoples in a collection that seeks to illuminate the racism and thoughtless colonisation of the prospectors and the State authorities that were blind to the impact on local communities would have seriously undermined the impact of this work. I hope I have succeeded.

Chrys Salt 2020

This collection is a gift to the First Nations peoples of the
Yukon, many of whom still strive
to regain the way of life they lost.

Whatever poems I have made of their stories,
or fashioned from my own experience of being there,
in the spirit of just exchange I give them back.

Thanks and Acknowledgements

As well as the many people in archives, museums and First Nation Cultural Centres that helped me with my research – especially Donna Darbyshire at the Yukon Archives in Whitehorse, and the Museum at Carcross – thanks are due to Philip and Lise Merchant who hosted us in Whitehorse, facilitated various trips and shared insights into the landscape and cultural history of the Yukon. Tizzy and Chuck Harborough who accommodated us in Seattle, to poet and writer Joanna Lilley who generously organised readings for me in Whitehorse and Dawson City; the Skookum Jim family and the Carcross/Tagish First Nation; my fellow-writers in The Brondesbury Group who have patiently sat through readings of the collection and offered valuable advice – and of course always to my husband, Richard Macfarlane, the best friend and 'roadie' any poet could have. Huge thanks are due to Creative Scotland for the generous Open Lottery funding that enabled my second trip to the Yukon and finally, to my publishers Ronnie Goodyer and Dawn Bauling at Indigo Dreams Publishing. Dawn's expert and kindly editorial eye has been invaluable. Indigo Dreams make such beautiful books, their care for their stable of writers is exemplary and their ongoing trust and support for my work has opened up so many opportunities – I can't thank them enough.

CONTENTS

Skookum Jim

and

The Klondike Gold Rush

Panning for words

Dip your pan
and dredge it in the stream.
Discard the rock,
it has no worth.
Next rubble roughened with the rasp
of too much thought
might have you fooled,
but tip it back,
it's poor stuff for your trade.
Now down to grit
your prospect's better now.
Sieve it, inspect it,
swill it round
then maybe in its settling
you'll find a tiny gleam
of gold dust in the silt,
the inkling of a seam.

Gold

They say The Han discovered it,
scooped it from bank and tributary,
swapped it like marbles and collected it,
tossed it in hand games carelessly,
too soft to hone, less currency
than fish, fur, berry, bone;
a lumpy yellow stone to them,
shiny and prettier, yes.

The Storyteller

He has an ear in every pie,
a dressing up box full of words.
'Wear this!' he says,
'the voice of caribou,
skin stretched
and scraped to thinness,
stitched with bone,
made fine with beadwork,
decorative quills,
a coat to dress your story in.

I try it on.

Or this,
the voice of Frog.
Be puppeteer.
Slip your hands in hers,
webbed fingers fitting like a glove.
Make songs for her,
spin dreams anew.

Or this,
the Raven's voice,
a trickster's voice
disguised,
transformed,
made otherwise.

Then from the bottom of his box
a voice I recognise,
a voice that lost its voice
in someone else's narrative,
of stolen land,
fishing and hunting grounds
mountains chewed up
and vomited.

It fitted me.

I wear my own voice now,
strut it inside the covers of a book.
String puppets for my songs,
revive some willing ghosts of words
to dance my stories on.

PART 1: SKOOKUM JIM AND THE FROG

Raven Song
Adapted from an original First Nation Legend

It started dark when only fire was bright
and World grew sick of bumping into things.
I heard inside a box,
inside a box,
inside a box,
inside a box
inside the smallest one,
an Old Man by The River kept The Light.

World wanted it and so I hatched a plan.
I changed into a needle from a pine
and when his granddaughter came to drink,
fingered her pathway down from tree to tree,
I jumped inside her darkling cup,
she drank and swallowed me.

I waited in her, grew and grew,
came into their house when time was due,
a human child I seemed to be,
my round black eyes invisible.
Wily I waited, learned the tongues of men,
until that Old Man loved me like a son.
I begged and begged just once,
to hold The Light, to see it shine.

So much by then he trusted me
he opened up the smallest box
to please,

and Lovely Light
leapt from it
like a fox.

I was Raven then before he knew.
I grabbed Light in my beak and flew and flew
straight up his smoke-hole to the waiting dark.

Light spilt and freckled darkness as I sped.
Orbs round and bold rolled out
for Sky to hold
and there was Light
so all could see the beauty of The World.

Keish's childhood 1850s

tight in a blanket
he rode on his mother
child of the Wolf Clan
Bear was his brother
ran where the moose ran
bronze brown and laughing
knew what his bones knew
before his arriving
tales of the Yukon
passed on with the telling
smelled the moon rising
before night was waking
saw big winds whisper
before leaves were shaking
whip crack of dawn light
first spring ice breaking
portent of snow slide
in the year's turning
tracked as a wolf might
the caribou's wandering
learned at his making
when words are spoken
there is no unsaying
when earth is broken
there is no returning.

Frog Song (1)

I was exhausted, desperate,
flailing at rock slide,
no escape,
no purchase on the slimy side.
Then scooped from mud and grit
saw my green watchfulness
as from afar, cupped in a furnace of strange hands,
my tongue protruded ready to touch his.

Then oh, release! A flight through light and air,
free fall, bright swill and cool anointing balm,
weed stroke in bubble dappled deeps,
my silk smooth element
washing the frantic moment clean.

He only hears me croak.
Would that his ear might catch
the nuances.
He did not hear me offer him my skin,
but stood for several moments on the bank
a mirrored shadow, gazing down
too big and strong he seemed for gentleness,
and then content to see me dive,
grew small and disappeared into the trees.

The Story

Ain't a year gone by, minding himself
out on the broad walk by some big hotel –
weren't the likes of Jim allowed in there them days –
this drunken fella falls careening out,
he comes at Jim all curse and kick and growl
calling him prairie nigger, muckleshoot
no reason in his head that Jim can see,
upshot he slits Jim open with his boot
and Jim's laid low, burning up like a forge,
sweat swilling outa him, bear rug heavy
as a bacon load. He's breathing slow,
can't get the tune of it. Owl's hooting for him
in the cedar tree. Now here's a thing,
now here's the strangest thing,
I'm telling this just how it's told to me,
in the wound – it's festering pretty bad –
Jim feels this tickling, nibbling slurp,
and that self same coast frog's supping on the rot!
Next day, and no explaining how, Jim's out there
brighter than fireweed fishing in the creek.

'prairie nigger, muckleshoot': derogatory slag for a First Nation person.
'Owl': many Native Americans considered owls to be symbols of death.

Frog Song (2)

He knew my glittering eyes from dreams ago.
His wound's bright mouth was closing
where I licked.
I stayed with him,
sang Frog Song on his bed,
nested in gifts of swan's-down,
silk thread, coloured beads –
how Frog was born of the last snowflakes,
how being small became a mountain
how he 'would live life like a story'
when the wound was clean,
passed on from mouth to mouth,
the tale of Skookum's Dream.

Frog Song (3)

When Raven stole The Sun
and day was made,
mine was a gift of Elements,
to pass from land to water,
enter dreams,
sing Frog Song in the ears of men.

I shine, I shimmer as in dreams I can.
I slip inside him secret as a wish,
lay sweetmeats at his door,
lead him in Woman Shape
through gilded rooms,
past glistering furniture,
show him a window pointing north,
a twisty trail, a mountain sliced to stairs,
arrows of water leaping red ravines,
uncharted ways, to salmon runs.
Set him by Hammer Water's child,
chit-chattering round rock in slips of light.
Give him a gold tipped walking stick,
bear meat, a pick, a cooking pan,
show him in weedy deeps
earth light and lantern shine
beneath dark wings of overhanging pine.

Love in Three Acts

Act 1
Meeting at Caribou Crossing

She'll sneak sly smiles at him,
her jet hair looping over cooking pots,
stitch trousers lined with fur
mittens of rabbit skin,
sew moccasins,
smoke tongues of caribou, his favourite.
Teach him to set traps for fish,
snare ptarmigan,
harvest berries, hunt like wolves.
He'll learn to pack a hundred pounds of bacon
up The Chilkoot Trail as well as any Indian.

She'll love his paler skin,
his thatch moustache, crag nose,
eyes blue as irises,
yearn for the tickle of his kiss.

He'll leave behind,
the orphaned boy in California,
rancher, marine, deserter, travelling man,
learn Tagish, tribal dances,
what their dreams foretold.
Bring nothing but The Fever left in him.
Find nothing yet but glints and promises.
Her sky becomes his sky,
her ways, his ways.

Her name is Shaaw Tláa
but he'll call her Kate.

Act 2
Family photograph: California 1898

Hair parted short and slick,
moustache clipped neat and tame
wing collar, waistcoat, peeking cuffs.
Hands round an ornamental cane.

Her mane a comely topknot now,
her posture plump and matronly,
a chain of nuggets loop across
a formal blouse of life worn patiently.

Perched on a pillar in a pretty frock
their brown skinned daughter holds a rose –
'George, Kate and Graphie. California',
The perfect family one might suppose.

Act 3
California 1899

She'll hang her nugget necklace on a tree,
run barefoot with their daughter in the woods,
spear red legged frogs, shoot off the heads
of rattlesnakes for fun,
trap squirrels for the cooking pot.

He'll appear in photographs without her,
bank his cash. Buy real estate, a motor car,
dine with the fashionable set,
feel lucky, stake more claims,
meet one more suited to his risen star.

She'll grow mad with drink and jealousy
in hotel corridors, smash down doors.
Get arrested. Make the newspapers.
'The dusky squaw man's savage spouse
crooning wild and warlike melodies,'

He'll rail against *'that woman's savage brawls,'*
file law suits, fight for custody,
marry his Yankee paramour,
send Kate empty handed home.

The Story

George Carmack and his Katie's gone some years,
prospecting up the Yukon in the wild
and Jim starts wondering where they've gotten to,
her being 'blood' him looking out for her.
Carmack could stake a claim on flour gold,
call a tiddler a Tagish Trout.
White men call him Squaw Man, Lying George,
now he's shacked up with Kate. Jim's fretting
so he builds a boat with nephew Charlie,
loads it up with stores, poles up The Tagish,
Windy Arm and over Lake Laberge.
No-one's seen 'em so they carry on
until hope of finding them's worn through.
Gets to Moosehide and they fetches up,
pleased as grizzlies in a berry patch
to see them after being away so long.
Been at a fish camp with some native folk,
up where the Yukon and the Klondike meet.
George says this white man Robert Henderson –
miner from Nova Scotia, smooth as mud –
has told him, white to white, there's 'colours' down
Gold Bottom Creek, asks George to pitch along
but wants 'no damned siwashes staking claim'.
Carmack ain't sure, he's panned down every creek,
found no gold there in paying quantities,
and anyway, don't like his attitude!
'Keeps his baccy and his pay dirt tight', says George,
'mean as a wolf is Robert Henderson.'

'Siwash': derived from the French 'sauvage', wild – A pejorative word for Native People. 'Pay dirt': ground containing ore in profitable quantities. 'Colours': traces of gold.

Salmon Song
George Carmack's Dream

When the last snowflakes fell
Frog came again,
then, as the season turned, Our Kind
grown big from fingerlings
to feed The River Folk.
Frog told us of her pact with Man,
how we must go
to find a dreamscape in a white man's head,
that we will have no tongue but glittering,
must enter in where mint-green water ran.
We came embossed with scales of gold,
equipped and shining for a dream she'd made,
our tails, gold rudders, nugget eyes,
fins laced with gold as fine as filigree.
The biggest of Our Kind we were,
deep bellied, golden with Frog's messages.
We muscled, surfaced,
swam where grayling shoaled,
appeared to him in leaping light,
darted askance when fingers reached
to catch the moment, keep it whole
as men in dreaming think they might.

We were not privy to his waking thought,
but in the gap that dreams slip through,
unmaking us, we saw him gaze
across the creek's bright course,
perplexed and wondering...

Tourist Tableau, Bonanza Creek 2017

The metal cut-outs are identical,
trousers tucked into boots,
wide miners' hats,
no telling which is white man, 'Indian'.
One waves his arms and pan aloft,
a second kneels, appears to pan the grass
the third looks on, his gold pan dangling.
The tourists' tableau misses everything –
the corn bright, dime sized nugget
found by accident,
the water, green with moss on which it ran,
amazement far too big for measurement,
jumping hallooing pounding feet,
bear steaks sizzling for a feast,
wet boots forgotten in their singing time,
of how they came to be here, desperate days,
empty gold pans, hunger, sucking slush,
journeys over numbing permafrost,
barren rivers, sodden underbrush.

How they slept sweetly on that day
rolled in their sleeping robes
as fire died,
dreams lulled by Frog Song,
Salmon prophesy.

Panning Bonanza Creek 2017

A man in an orange shirt,
floppy shorts pans in the river
to his nippy knees.
A tall guy in an anorak,
hood up against the flies, scoops mud.
A girl with back pack, boots and spectacles,
hunches in concentration on the bank.
She scrutinises grit, pokes, lobs it back.

We watch them play their game of chance,
dip, sieve, scan, dip. Persist.
Perhaps it's just a tourist's exercise
although their rapt attention
might say otherwise.
It's just one nugget after all, just one,
a fortune that the nosing diggers missed.

Stones from Bonanza Creek 2017

Knives squelch through bear flesh,
water dithers over river bed,
cackle of tinder, spittle of green wood
flollop of severed skin, a plip of blood,
sputter of bear fat, splat of landed fish,
slither of gutted innards in the mud.

Then something found, rare, unmistakable.
Not these poor dull relations in my hand,
but a rich brother from another age,
dressed in the future, promising the earth.

PART 2: THE KLONDIKE GOLD RUSH

Gold! Gold! Gold! Gold!

Before that steamer docked
we just got on with it,
baked bread, cut timber, landed fish
shopped in Bonmarché, paid off loans.

It took one headline to upend the times,
inject sane men with lunacy,
men off the boat, exhausted, jubilant,
fortunes in sacks, bags, blankets, coffee cans.
Lives opened up to possibility.

Joe left his job,
said he'd no time for that,
some story about gofers
that could gnaw through permafrost,
A Klondike bicycle!
A house as light as air you could pack flat
with iron stove and double bed.
'Who's mining who?' I said.

The city emptied, ovens cooled.
Store keepers abandoned shops,
meat, cheese on counters left to rot,
drivers abandoned street cars on the spot.
Our Mayor resigned,
clerks, policemen, long shore men,
my dad, our next door neighbour, friends
mortgaged their houses, took out loans,
cashed in the future for no turning back.

Joe bought his outfit,
flour, bacon, beans, booked a passage
on some filthy barge, so jammed with gear
I marvelled it could float!

News leaked back
of avalanches, foundered boats,
men whipped at posts, and shot for thieving,
horrid tales,
dead men and rotting horses
on the Trails.

I wrote, I wrote, but no reply,
of promised riches nothing came.
Our Billy cried for him,
asked 'how long, where and why?'
Had nothing but a stupid photograph
Joe in his shirt sleeves posing with the dog,
fake snow, a painted mountain back drop,
pines, low sun,
foot on a prop sledge, shouldering a gun.

The Fever

he found a fleck of it inside a fish
a twinkle in the blood
glint became nuggets
pictured in a book
he mined the flaked opacity of flesh
dug his knife to bedrock skeleton
followed a song the fishbone sang
flew the mind's eye
to lake and glacier
leant pick and spade
on phantom rock
scooped silt from salmon grounds
sluiced to a yellowness of corn
won't speak its name
for fear in naming it were lost
eyes wide and fierce
hand clamped across a scream
held out its pure deep shining
at arm's length
stock still with knowing
that this, this is,
this is the spinning moment
the last ace poised
above a Royal Flush
when fire kept its tongue
trees dipped in molten sun
water made honey knew
this second held
the future in its breathing out
would open at the bookmark
of his coming back.

Song of the wise Chieftain

When they came like the Mosquito
Chieftain told Raven
'Raven, fly away
and store our songs
for no-one else must sing them.'
When Hammer Water spoke
of chattering tongues
on salmon weirs and hunting grounds
Chieftain asked Moon
to light three fires to save them.
When Mountain spoke
of steeps and hollows eaten out
in one short fickle season
Chieftain asked Bear
to store their memories
until times came good to share them.

Bennett Lake

Easy for us landing on the lake.
Our pilot helps us off along a wing,
to a damp strand where men made
camp, built crazy boats, sweating

against the clock; whip-sawed green wood,
swore, nailed and tarred, before blue ice
thwarted their passage, strength and food
ran out, betting against a loaded dice

each frenzied hammer blow
might bring them closer to their goal.
The landscape's different now.
Pines flourish down the slopes, a shawl

of silence drapes the lake's perimeter.
Here their rowdy tented city sprang,
rations, boots, outfits, sleds heaped where
unflustered sand arcs gold along

the shore and over heedless stones,
over the lies of easy maps,
the lottery of hope, their broken bones
indifferent water laps.

What the lookout saw
(Beaver Mountain 1897)

The placid Yukon winds its arms
round inlets, reed beds, stranded isles,
glacial silt washed down from mountains
to the river's lip,
sheer sand banks undercut by currents,
pocked with swallows' nests.

He's standing where he always stands,
high on the warty outcrop,
look-out for bark canoes,
graceful and marvellously light,
skimming towards his village with their wares –

but not for this, this
silence shredded to a din,
these shrieking clouds,
hurled spume, this smash,
this loud flotilla on the water snake.
How could there be so many in the world?

Swift on his moccasins
he scrambles down.
He shouts in the fields,
he shouts in the fish camp.
He runs like the hare to tell them
that the white man comes again,
lights fires on their land,
takes fish for dog food,
scares the moose
cuts down trees,

trample the sweet-grass,
makes rivers run backwards,
turns mountains inside out.

'Until our fallen warriors return,'
the wise Chief says,
'we will be moose calves in a land of wolves.'

A Sinking

How could I not remember how it was?
Rain whipped our hull like punishment.
Waves keen, short, steep and merciless,
eyes blizzard-blind, deck lashed
with icy tides, and all gushed in.
I screamed 'more wood, more wood'
but saw the boiler door stood wide,
the hatch with all our outfits stashed,
awash and open.
We were going down.

How could I not remember it?
The pilothouse still floating,
O my God, so cold.
Fingers with their own mind hanging on,
the sodden flag of me
swept out and back, out, back
stiff, slack
so cold, dear God so cold.
Better to drop, than hang until I dropped,
I was so small inside it all
but still my treacherous hands clung on.

Then in a sudden stilly aftermath,
a bark canoe,
my father's ghost I thought
come to redeem the last of me,

I think I dropped my coat and shoes on board
before I tried to swim for it ...

Caribou

A teenage boy,
his trapper's hat jewelled with mosquitoes,
has shot a caribou.
We brake our camper to investigate.

'We are Gwitch'in,' says his father,
defensive to the bone.
He shuffles from foot to foot,
studies the tolerant stones.

The soft majestic head is propped
below the highway on the verge,
branchy antlers tangle with the brush,
glass marble eyes reflect
old songs and dances,
tales of herds and hunts.

We help them heave the carcass to their truck.
They beam at us,
it's first names, photographs.
This kill will feed their family for a month.

On a clear night you might see the lad
caught in a moonlit clearing at Old Crow,
alive and sacred in his hand
the heart he shares with the caribou.

Black Bear

Driving due north
we spot her on the verge
foraging for ants and dandelion,
no berries yet to fatten her.

She's cuddly, big as a human,
soft round ears erect,
button eyes sewn close
over a long furred snout.

She chomps and rummages
in lovage, fox-tail, plucks at
fireweed with prehensile lips –
then head askance and curious

lumbers towards our lay-by,
pads around the car,
snuffles the radiator,
head butts the bonnet and peers in.

We're still as rabbits on a hill,
ears cocked for predators
in case a twitch of a hand or eye
alerts her to our presence and alarms –

then she ambles off towards
the forest gloom, turns, glares at us,
humped, dangerous, claws glinting
like gang-land razors in the July sun.

Dyea 2017
The ghost town at the foot of The Chilkoot Pass

There's no one left to speak for it
but stories of a past it scarcely owns,

unless these rotting stumps
that march like standing stones
across the grass,
could spool back time,
resurrect the wharf,
stanchion by stanchion,
plank by flexing plank.

This hull, that bares its dead bird ribs to air
could borrow boughs from trees,
raise phantoms sharpened to a former shape,
take to the water, disgorge on the staithe
havocs of gaunt men doubled up with gear.

These scattered timbers in the fern,
fashion false frontages of restaurants,
meat stores, laundries, trading posts,
plump feather pillows, fill up steaming plates
with moose heart, bacon, Hangtown Fry,
glasses with liquor in the raucous bars.

Nothing remains
but what the mind's eye resurrects
from random clues and photographs,
signage for tourists pointing down long fields,
at water, sky and nothing there
to flesh the bones of this dead city's ghosts.

Slide Cemetery, Dyea 2017
Palm Sunday Avalanche 1898

On tidal flats in Dyea now,
are fields and fields of irises.
I think of Flanders and the poppies there,
wonder what strange memorial are these
for young men swallowed by an avalanche,
and now lie in this foreign field
that is forever none of them –
grave markers tilted
under flat leafed pine,
names elbow deep in fern,
stone scoured by rain and time –
men who in one demented summer came
from Kansas, Minnesota, Maine,
kitted with picks and spades,
not guns for victory.
Told they would pluck gold,
from rivers 'quick as raspberries',
were fed a false prospectus
like those other dead.

James Edward Doran 1898
John Morgan, Daniel Molinnan,
George Risser, C P Harris,
Walter Chapper, Thomas Culleden
more and more young men.
Palm Sunday, April 1898,
these and the eloquence of irises.

The Chilkoot Pass

We scramble up The Pass in single file,
between the berries and the brush,
each careful foot secured on grit and shale,
tree roots, broken branches, rolling cone.

On wider paths we squeeze aside
for serious walkers kitted out with back packs,
panniered dogs and proper boots,
trekking the Trail right to the end,

like those who came a century ago
need, greed and hunger in their bones
so deep it drove them on against all odds,
bitten by blizzards, flesh grown gangrenous

to claw at hope in mindless wastes of snow -
or gasping for air under an avalanche,
a longed-for letter hugged against the heart,
'Billy does well at school. How fast they grow.'

It's now a hikers' route, just manageable.
We grabble over boulders, edge sheer drops,
afraid we'll miss our footing, fall...
'dear love we will be reunited soon, I know.'

He wishes for the Internet...

'what if
my words could on some quick wind fly,
your reply be immediate.
If photographs of home
could wing through air
across this wilderness
arrive warmed through
or better still, I could appear
an apparition in our house,
and moving, speaking,
see our children play,
show you this queue of misery,
behind, above me,
hardly human, grim
corpses of horses
we have trodden on.
Could tell you eye to eye
how absence feels
how every day I think of you,
tell you however harsh the way
there's nothing's worse than coming
empty handed home.

I write so many letters dear,
receive so few....'

Five Finger Rapids

She growls, sprays, gorges, lashes out,
spatters her walls with spittle,
hungry still.

A brave man then to dare her ravening,
rather than hump gear, boats and outfits
across the land route to the other side.
Some, eyes fixed on early chance,
gritted their bones,
and ran the gauntlet of the famished tide.

The lucky ones made battered landfall.
Others gulped down by hungry cataracts,
savaged by rocks and never found.

A little story this,
a nugget rescued from one man's despair.
A French prospector on the flood
lost everything, boat wrecked
food, tools, stove, blankets, everything,
but salvaged in a locket round his neck,
shown off to everyone,
a gold strand of his baby daughter's hair.

Chipmunk above Five Ringer Rapids

We watch him munch, pouch seeds,
discard and spray the hulls,
beneath the forest's eaves,
and wonder if his stripy ancestors ate lunch
above the greedy madness of the age
just getting on with being chipmunks
in the leaves?

Grand Forks Hotel 1899

Wind rips stout canvas from the carts,
yammers at tent ribs, snarls outside the door,
hurls dust and flailing debris down the walls.
Grit spits along the broad walk spitefully.
Small windows peak through grime,
at horses neighing in the dark,
up to their fetlocks in the stinking mud.
Wind yowls, thin huskies howl
in makeshift kennels at the back. Packers,
prospectors, trackers, good-time girls
laugh, pout, drink, flirt, grow loud,
cigar smoke thick as soup, furls up
from fingers rimed and cracked with toil,
air gorged with sweat and dust, rich scents
of stewing moose heart, bacon, beans,
big talk of fortunes made and lost,
failed grubstakes, pay dirt, gain and cost
a man who boiled his boots for broth,
and died of hunger on The Chilkoot Pass.

*'grubstakes': money or materials given to prospectors in return for a share in
anything they found.*

The road to Dawson 2017

The husky's eyes were open
startling blue,
legs splayed as if running with a sled,
not a mark on him,
and beautiful.
We parked up, crossed the road.
'He's all I've got,' she wailed,
'I've nobody...'
But not to us,
the sky, some deaf or absent God,
the Universe.
I stroked the thin wool of her coat,
but she was comfortless.
She stared down at her dog,
shook, shook and shook her head
then haltingly, through tears and snot
said she'd been fishing in the creek,
the dog ran off,
she'd heard a car,
a thump, a yelp,
came to investigate.

We helped her lay
the limp grey body in her truck,
soft, heavy as a sack of sand, still warm –
then without a word of thanks
she headed back to Dawson
down that hopeless road.

Riding shotgun 2017

Journey in a float 'plane

'I'm riding shotgun,' he insists,
heaves his bulk into the tiny plane,
squats by the pilot in the front.
The drawl's American. Tells us
he drives a haulage truck back home.
His fierce wife squeezes in beside us
in the back. She's a correction officer,
not to be crossed – this flight
has been his dream she says,
so do we mind?
We say we don't. Of course we do.
Not quite as we'd imagined it,
squashed in a flimsy capsule,
no bigger than a family car,
with these just in it for the ride,
a box to tick, a story in the bar.

The Chilkoot Pass from the air

Clouds shred, drift, fray
above us, past us, under us,
smoke white against empyrean blue.

Goats pose on dizzying ledges,
graze between alabaster
troughs of snow.

Sun glances off Lalique,
spits off the glaciers
in arcs of fire.

We're fragile as a butterfly,
pitching on tides
of up-draught, undertow.

Our pilot ill-informed, but genial,
spiels through our head sets, indicates
The Pass below, The Golden Stairs,

a thin black thread that snakes up ice,
too far from the story anyway
to slip inside their skins from here;

the crippling climb on climb on climb,
the heft of iron and rations bending them,
the sheer hewn stairs, the stiff rope banister.

Robert Service's cabin, Dawson City 2017

The stage is set
with oil lamp, tea pot, typewriter,
books, photographs, an old guitar.

He's just stepped
out for air,
a ballad's dumpty dum
rhyming with footsteps on
a wooded walk
and yet
he never read
the Dawson City daily
on that desk,
fed the Klondike stove,
stacked that wood store
tidied up that bed,
sharpened those pencils,
never wore
those pristine snow shoes,
hanging on a hook,
that shirt and waistcoat
never his.

Outside a costumed actor
spouts his verse
minted from gossip
of mining veterans,
'whooping it up' in a saloon
until their fanciful embroidery
obscured the woeful fabric of the cloth.

Few warming logs,
or happy ends
for Sam McGee,
but red in greed and blood,
frozen horses
fed to skinny dogs,
in their turn,
eaten by famished men.

A Call Girl's Tale: Grand Forks Hotel 1890s

Ain't much to us to splay our legs
and some of us struck luck – poor ginks
just gotta spend, Cad Wilson got a belt
worth fifty thousand dollars for her time.
Another had her bathtub filled with wine!
Tall as the oblong dark outside he was,
had on a plaid shirt, gaudy, bright with checks,
a miners' hat decked off with crimson trim,
a watch chain dangling nuggets off like fish.
I showed some leg and pushed my bodice down –
us girls ain't picky when it comes to gold!
Comes in like he was home, pulls out his poke –
him an Indian in there and bold –
then smiling like he knows the whole of it
empties a heap of nuggets on the bar,
eyes on 'em hungry as wolves after caribou.
'Plenty, gold, plenty plenty gold' says he,
enough I swear to buy the whole damn town!
'Now I'm the first son of a Tagish Chief,
don't gain no access to a white man's house,
packed white man's outfits up The Chilkoot Pass,
don't gain no access to a white man's world...'
Belinda pours a tot to oil his tale.
He sips with sly, deliberate savouring,
lowers his voice, pauses the longest pause…
'I guess you want to know about the gold?'
Tells us this story of a Helper Frog,
how dreams come true, if you can read 'em right,
how meanness never did a fella good,
and no man said a word, for no man could.

The Gold Rush Museum, Seattle 2017

Fake nuggets, mock displays
of banks and stores.
Photos of horses, sleds and dogs.
Miners in mukluks, parkas, mitts,
'Indian' packers humping gear
across their stolen land for pay.

Hotel Seattle's not too far from there,
the story goes that Skookum Jim got drunk,
threw gold and bank notes
from the balcony,
watched white men on the pavement down below
grab at the fluttering air,
snatch nuggets from the fingers of their friends.

Outside the museum doors
police lock bicycles
to stem a baying tide of balaclavas.
A paramedic bathes a woman's eyes
red raw from pepper spray.
The slogan on her banner reads
Immigrants Go Home.

Mountain Voices

So used they were to broken things,
smashed oil lamps, wine jars,
rattled urns, the creak of houses,
tumbling masonry,
they just shrugged off the portents
of a mountain's rage,
repaired their fallen walls
and soldiered on.

Those who could read the writing in Spring wind,
sun's scribbled messages on ice,
told the prospectors it was dangerous,
warned of a snowpack in the mountain's throat,
before it raised its mighty voice and spoke.

So when Vesuvius spewed its guts,
and two millennia on a slice of snow
broke loose from natures moorings,
smothering everything,
too late in either case
to call for gods, too sudden
for the moment's fending off.

Some were found curled to foetuses,
or fused together in a last embrace.
Some frozen in a running shape,
or curled like cats asleep
heads on their forearms
under ash or snow,
perplexed perhaps to hear their mountain roar
before the snow or lava outran everyone.

Do we learn anything from history,
the stranded polar bear, the rising sea?

When writing this I found a photograph,
an unnamed man in glasses,
balding, elderly.
He holds against a sky blue shirt,
a plaster cast –
the body of a child from Herculaneum,
hands splayed across the tiny back,
so tenderly
you'd think the child
and his heart might break.

Coda

Land is not my school, my history,
my land was never disembowelled for gain,

nor have I roots grown down so deep in it
that in my bones I know it to be mine.

I am not subject to The Season's laws,
nor do they govern where I stay or go.

I have no Homeland to be taken back,
no drum to beat that no one listens to,

no shaman to recover what I've lost,
no Frog to heal or teach me to be wise,

no Elders to pass on the lore, learned
from the throat songs of my ancestors.

Language was not stolen from my mouth,
nor did my children grow up separate.

I cannot know how loss makes warriors
or hold a potlatch for your ancient grief,

but fashion stories with a poets tongue,
your stories walking in my skin,

make them anew and give them back,
of rights, of heritage, your living land.

From 1902 onwards the First Nations of the Yukon campaigned for action to address the racism, dispossession, unabated resource extraction, and poverty arising from the loss of the traditional life-style that had sustained them:

"The only way we feel we can have a future is to settle our land claim ... that will return to us our lost pride, self-respect and economic independence." Chief Elijah Smith. 1973.

It took the Federal Government 90 years to respond but between 1993 and 2005 land settlement and self-government agreements were finalised with 11 of the 14 Yukon First Nations.

In 2007 most nations adopted the United Nation's Declaration on The Rights of Indigenous People – an agreement that recognises indigenous rights to self-government, land, equality and language as well as basis human rights – Canada only signed in 2016 after a change of federal government.

The term First Nation was adopted in 1970 as the word 'Indian' is considered to be offensive. I have used it only when relevant to context and the period.

Afterword

I dreamed the only gold was sun,
Frog led where Mountain swallowed snow
made flowers from ice
breathed sweet wind through the dead
who rose, went home,
forgetting why they'd come,
that on the Yukon's lazy bank
Greed lounged with sandwiches
and fished
then catching nothing, fell asleep.

NOTES

Page 12: Gold
The Han or Hwëch'in: a First Nation people of the Yukon.

Page 17: Keish's childhood 1950s
Skookum Jim Mason, whose First Nation name was Keish was the first son of a Tagish Chief. In the mid 1880's he worked as a packer carrying heavy supplies for white miners over the Chilkoot Pass – one of the long, dangerous routes to the Gold Fields. He was nicknamed Skookum Jim because of his great strength – Skookum meaning big and strong in Chinook coastal language.

Page 18: Frog Song (1)
The Frog symbolises wealth and abundance. When Frog's tongue touches another creature, it represents the sharing of knowledge and power.

Page 21: Frog Song (3)
Hammer Water is a First Nation name for The Klondike River. Rabbit Creek, where Keish and his party made their rich discover, is one of its tributaries.

Page 22: Meeting at Caribou Crossing
George Carmack was a deserter from the U.S. Marine Corps in 1882, and subsequently lived among the Tagish Indians in the Yukon Valley. He was hired with Keish to pack supplies over The Chilkoot Pass for rich prospectors. George fell in love with Keish's sister Shaaw Tláa who also packed supplies over the Trail. He came to find gold.

Page 24: California 1899
In 1900 George married Marguerite Saftig Laimee, a stylish woman of questionable repute. His common law marriage to Kate was not recognised by the courts. She returned home penniless and was subsequently written out of George's story.

Page 25: The Story
Robert Henderson will live to regret his racism when Carmack's party don't share news about their rich strike as was customary among the prospectors.

Page 26: Salmon Song
George interprets his dream to mean he has more chance of catching salmon than prospecting with Robert Henderson, so sets of with his small party to fish in Rabbit Creek.

Page 27: Tourist Tableau, Bonanza Creek 2017
Who found the first nugget in Rabbit Creek (renamed Bonanza) remains a matter of dispute. It has been suggested that as Carmack had registered the claim – as a white man the only one who could – he took the credit to help erase links to his native family that he abandoned after striking it rich.

Page 31: Gold! Gold! Gold!
The Portland Steamer docked in Seattle July 17th 1897 disgorging 68 prospectors who shared more than a ton of gold found in the river now known as the Yukon. It was that find, and a headline in The Seattle Post-Intelligencer, that started The Klondike Gold Rush.

Page 39: Caribou
The Gwich'in creation story tells how Gwich'in people and the caribou separated from a single entity and share the same heart. Gwich'in means 'people of the caribou.' For centuries First Nation people in Northern Canada have relied on caribou for food and clothing.
Old Crow is a tiny First Nation Community in the far north of the Yukon Territories. It is only accessible by air.

Page 45: Five Finger Rapids
Five Finger Rapids was a major obstacle on the route to the Gold Fields. Many prospectors ended up in the water as they tried to negotiate their homemade craft down the narrow steep sided torrent.

Page 47: Grand Forks Hotel 1899

Grand Forks Hotel was a prominent roadhouse much used by prospectors at the time of the Gold Rush.

Page 50: The Chilkoot Pass from the air

To be allowed to enter the Yukon, Canadian Mounties guarding the frontier required prospectors take one ton of food and equipment with them, so they were prepared to survive their onward journey. This meant many trips on a hazardous, near vertical climb up steps carved out of the glacier: The Golden Stairs.

Page 57: Coda

A potlatch: a ceremony practiced among indigenous groups of the Northwest coastal regions of Canada to celebrate births, give names, conduct marriages, mourn the loss of a loved one, or pass rights from a Chief to his eldest son.

The Canadian Government has apologised for many abuses committed over a 150 years when around 150,000 First Nation children were forcibly separated from their parents and sent to residential schools run by the church ostensibly to 'assimilate' them. They were taught their belief systems were wrong, were forbidden to speak their language or exercise their culture.

Bibliography:

Good Time Girls of The Alaska Yukon Gold Rush: Lael Morgan *(Epicenter Press, 1999)*

Sam Steele: The Wild West Adventures of Canada's most Famous Mountie: Holly Quan *(Altitude Publishing, 2003)*

Life Lived Like a Story: Julie Cruikshank in collaboration with Angela Sidney, Kitty Smith and Annie Ned. *(University of Nebraska Press 1994)*

George Carmack: Man of Mystery who set off The Klondike Gold Rush: James Albert Johnson *(Epicenter Press 2001)*

Women of the Klondike: Frances Backhouse *(Whitecap Books 15th Anniversary Edition, 2010)*

Hammerstones. A History of The Tr'ondëk Hwëch'in: Helene Dobrowolsky *(Tr'ondëk Hwëch'in, 2014)*

The Klondike Quest: Pierre Berton *(The Boston Mills Press, 1997)*
The Klondike Stampede: Tappan Adney *(UBC Press, 1994)*

Indigo Dreams Publishing Ltd
24, Forest Houses
Cookworthy Moor
Halwill
Beaworthy
Devon
EX21 5UU
www.indigodreams.co.uk